THE SATIRIST

The Satirist

Prose Poems

Caleb Bouchard

Suburban Drunk Press
2023

ISBN: 979-8-218-12860-9

Cover design and author photo: Aubrie Sofala

Cover art: "The Anarchist" by Félix Vallotton

Email: calbchrd@gmail.com

Instagram: @calebbouchard

For Gus and Aubrie

Table of Contents

THE SATIRIST

The Satirist

After the police officer pulled me over, the first thing he said was, "Are you the satirist?" I said, "I certainly am not. I don't think I've ever even met a satirist." The officer unfolded a photograph from his pocket, studied it, then pinned a glare on me. He showed me the picture. "You're telling me you don't know who this is?" He showed me the photograph. It was my cousin, Marcus. We looked almost identical, though I was a bit heavier at the time, and Marcus had hints of a scraggly beard whereas I've always been clean shaven. We hadn't spoken or seen each other in years, ever since he went off to art school and I took a job at the local bank. I almost explained all this to the officer, but caught myself before spilling the beans. Instead I said, "That guy looks malnourished. Look at me. We're not the same. What do you want with a lowly satirist, anyway?" The officer said, "He wrote an off-color play about a friend of the mayor." "Really? Was it a comedy or a tragedy?" I said. "I can't disclose that," the officer said. "What is Mar— the satirist, I mean, charged with?" I said. The officer seemed distracted. He was fanning his flashlight in the backseat of my car, where my pickleball gear lay buried in the floorboards. Above us, a chopper with a search light sliced its way through the night sky. My palms started to dampen, so I asked if I could continue on my way. The officer said, "One more thing." He pulled out a colorful greeting card which had a drawing of a bright-eyed porcupine holding a red balloon. "It's my daughter's birthday tomorrow. You'd be doing me a big favor if you could write something. Make it witty."

Elvis at NYU

An Elvis impersonator was invited to give a one-day graduate seminar at NYU. During the talk, Elvis demonstrated such techniques as the powerhouse knee drop, the one-arm windmill, and the iconic sneer, which, Elvis emphasized, was the essence of the King. "If you can't master the sneer, you can forget about the rest, mama. It's the curtain that rises before the play." Elvis also showed the packed auditorium the proper method of wiping off sweat and flicking it into the audience with grace and poise, a maneuver that made women go wild but which few impersonators could authentically replicate. During the Q&A session, a student in the third row asked Elvis if he could give a tutorial on the "Hound Dog" hip shake, but Elvis shook his head. He explained that the hip shake was a move Elvis neither invented nor perfected; it was more of a marketing ploy to sell movie tickets rather than a genuine artistic expression. At the end of the workshop, one of the deans of the university — Elvis forgot which college or school she served — presented him with an honorary doctorate in performance studies, to which Elvis responded, "Oh, this ain't a performance, mama. This is life."

Slippage

A love letter tacked on a refrigerator slips from the grip of the magnet and lands inside the fridge, among the leftovers, uncooked meat, and vegetables. The love letter grows cold over time, absorbing all the pungent smells of the dwelling Tupperware. Grimy spinach. Stale soup. Chili caked in a layer of discolored fat. The letter's edges curdle and the penned words blanch in solidarity with the forsaken dishes. This continues until the words have completely faded into vapor. The page is empty, and somewhat crepey.

Coughing Fit

A man picked up a half-smoked cigarette from the ground outside of a pawn shop. He inhaled, savoring the sweet tobacco. As he released the smoke, the man turned into a zebra. He spotted his reflection in a shop window and galloped and whinnied with joy. Dropping the lit cigarette, he charged home to tell his family he had just been promoted.

A plastic bag blowing through the wind then picked up the still-burning cigarette. The bag inhaled and immediately collapsed into a series of side-splitting coughs. At the intersection sat a family of plastic bags in a large SUV. The little boy and little girl plastic bags pointed, quivering, asking their plastic parents, "What kind of weather is that?"

Small Spaces

Yesterday evening, my wife came home with a candle a coworker had given her. The candle didn't have a hokey name like candles usually do, like *Seaside Kisses* or *Harvest Season Hayride*. It didn't have much of a design, either, like the candles you see in big box stores. My wife set it on the TV console and we had dinner — a recipe I like to call *eggroll in a bowl*. We talked about traffic and fast approaching work deadlines, and the way life seems to sucker punch you sometimes. After dinner we changed into our pajamas and sat in front of the TV. "Want to light that candle?" I asked her, and she said yes. I got up and fumbled with the candle and lighter. When I settled back on the couch, I noticed the color in my wife's eyes had changed — they had gone from a deep, dark brown to an almost translucent gray. If they were any lighter, I thought, I'd be looking straight through her brain, to the back side of her skull. Before I could say anything, though, she turned up the volume on her favorite show, and as we sat back she raised her foot onto my lap. "You don't have to..." she said, but I already picked up her signal. I didn't mind, anyway. Every now and then I'd sneak a glance at her eyes. They had changed again. Now, ghostly trails of smoke rose within her irises, embedded with the gray.

After the episode, I drew in a deep breath through my nose, but smelled nothing. "Do you smell the candle?" I said. "I do," she said, then offhandedly added, "I think it's one of those candles that is meant for small spaces." I got up and took the candle over to the breakfast nook. "Smaller," said my wife. I walked into the kitchen and nestled the candle in between the coffee machine and the air fryer. "Try again," she said from the living room. I went all over the house trying to find the perfect spot. The bathroom, the bedroom, her office, my study. *Nope. Not quite. Meh. I don't think so.* The candle seemed to pulsate as I held it. Eventually, I stuffed my feet into some old sandals and went out to the backyard, to the old dog house adjacent to the back porch. It had been out of commission ever since Gristle, our Golden Retriever, had passed a year earlier. I placed the candle on the dirt floor of the dog house, and crouched there, waiting to smell some sort of beautiful aromatic orchestra. Whiskey and cedar. Gardenia and lavender. Something, anything, to arouse me from my odorless milktoast existence. I waited several minutes, but no dice. Back in the house, I found my wife asleep in our bedroom; a luminescent glow projected through her closed eyelids. In them, I saw plums of stardust, enigmatic constellations, sequences of dreams I had from before I was born. As I drifted off to sleep, I thought I heard a tiny animal howling, small as a single flame.

Elvis Pays His Respects

An Elvis impersonator drove down to Pembroke Pines, Florida, to preside over a funeral. The weather was so sticky, so warm and gooey, it reminded him of a peanut butter and banana sandwich. The branches of palm trees slumped towards the scorching hot ground, their leaves bloated from sunlight. The heaviness in the air made Elvis antsy. At the church, the dead man's wife cried on Elvis's black suede jumpsuit, which was decorated with golden studs on the torso and outer leg seams. The dead man's daughter, a plump woman in her forties, handed Elvis some prepared remarks, which he read at the beginning of the service. Less than a dozen people filled the creaky wooden rows, their crepey skin the color of pork rinds. He read from the prepared remarks, which extolled the wholesome virtues and values of the dead man, how he loved his family more than all of the riches in the world. Elvis then opened it up for eulogies from the audience. A bald man with a green fanny pack blurted, "Mort owed me five hundred dollars." He then turned to the dead man's wife. "I expect restitution, Cynthia."

After the service, the frail, wrinkled pallbearers (friends the dead man had made through bingo night at Hooters) carried the casket out to the graveyard. As the dead man's body was lowered into the ground, Elvis sang an a cappella version of "I'll Remember You," from the 1966 American musical comedy *Spinout*. Everyone stared at the gaping hole in the earth as he sang. They were still lowering the casket into the ground when Elvis finished singing. The dead man's daughter gestured to him, ordering him to sing another, but he had been paid only to do one song. Instead, he contorted his body into the shape of a white crane and executed a smooth, sweeping kick, like a seagull flying over a sandy shoreline at daybreak. Kung fu was always free of charge.

The Yellow of Gray

In the town of Gray, everything was yellow. It wasn't always this way. Things were once gray in Gray. The townspeople were quite pleased with their coin-colored pastures, their graphite farmhouses and chapels. And then a new mayor was elected — he was from a big city and owned a pewter summer home by the leaden lake. He claimed the town didn't have enough local color, and so he had everything painted yellow, from buildings and bridges to the trees and horses in the field. He even arranged for the lake to be treated with harmful chemicals, which killed the fish and changed the water's color to a strange parmesan shade. Before long, the fog-faced citizens of Gray put pressure on the town council for a public meeting, which took place in the mustard-colored city hall. One by one, the townspeople — wearing charcoal slacks and flinty flannel shirts — approached the bumblebee-hued microphone and aired their complaints to the mayor and aldermen.

"All of this yellow hurts my eyes," one elderly woman bemoaned. "Yellow goes against all of the values we hold dear in Gray," a man with a silver beard denounced. "It just doesn't belong." The meeting went on for more than an hour. A child of three or four years old closed out the public hearing by saying, "The yellow makes Mommy sad. She drinks a lot more Mommy juice now. Please bring back the gray of Gray. We miss it dearly." The mayor, wearing a buttermilk suit, defended his actions by saying the most naturally beautiful things in life were yellow. Sunflowers. Freshly squeezed lemonade. Long summer days. He argued that an appreciation for things such as these helped one live life on a deeper, more fulfilled level. His colorful words, however, failed to penetrate the shadowy mood in the room, which seemed filled with the tastelessness of arsenic.

The Complication

When I awoke from the operation, the doctor said my transplant
had been successful, but not without complications. "You see," he
said, "when we opened you up and looked at the area where a heart
should be, there was no heart in there at all, but instead an old,
half-opened soup can. So, we checked the label and I sent one of
my externs down to the bodega to get a can of tomato soup. We
drained the soup into a pot and from there it was smooth sailing."
As he spoke, I nodded, lifting a hand to cover my reddening
cheeks. I suppose I should have let them know about my old can
before the procedure. Heck, I could have brought a can or two of
my own. Before the doctor left, I asked if there was any soup left on
the burner, playing dumb. I could hear the nurses slurping behind
the curtain.

The Eyes Above

The trees in the grove behind our home have eyes. We don't know
what to call this species of tree, and yet, we aren't bothered by
them. Now it is early spring, and the eyelids are pink and tough,
just beginning to bud. By May, they will bloom and blossom,
fanning themselves out to reveal richly colored irises, crystalline
blue and profound brown. For some reason, green irises are hard
to come by in this region. I've read they fare better in the
hinterlands.

We will enjoy looking at the eyes throughout the summer, eyeing
the eyes which are eyeing us, opening and closing seemingly
without a care. We could pluck them from their branches, toss
them into a stew, but refrain from doing so. They bring us so much
color, so much comfort. They are like unobstructive family
members, letting us go along with our lives while admiring us from
a distance.

Towards autumn, inevitably, the lids will begin to blister and
shrivel. The irises will turn milky, the pupils will begin to careen
and wander, lose focus. They will plunk to the ground, one by one,
at first. By Thanksgiving, though, the old raisiny eyes will blanket
the grass beneath the trees, leaving the branches bare, needle-like.
It's the natural cycle of the seasons, we suppose, but it's still
difficult to watch. Father, especially, hates having to rake them up,
while the winter sun obscures itself behind ashen, faceless clouds.

Diagnostic

A woman woke up one morning with a lump in her armpit the size of a tennis ball. The lump had a funny feeling about it, tough and fuzzy. She told her husband about the lump, concluding, "Maybe it really *is* a tennis ball." Her husband said, "Could be. You know Roy, from church? They found a softball in his shin a few days ago. It was in the weekly newsletter." The woman drove herself to the doctor, who examined her with skepticism. "Tennis balls tend to be over-diagnosed," the doctor said with squinty eyes. "Most likely, it's a golf ball, or a clementine. Let's do an x-ray and get to the bottom of this." A nurse led her into the x-ray room where a technician provided the woman with a lead apron. As the woman put on the apron, she remembered how she and her husband played tennis on an almost daily basis, early on in their courtship. They were energetic then, tan and thin. Their skin was dewey and blemishless, their parts weren't wrinkled, didn't swing and sag. They could barely take their hands off each other, they were so filled with verve and vigor. The same couldn't be said today. She missed those carefree, jubilant times. As the technician ran the test, the woman tried to push the doctor's doubtful comments out of her mind. She hoped with every fiber that it was in fact a tennis ball in her armpit. *Please, Lord,* she thought, *I'd do anything for a tennis ball. Not a golf ball or a clementine. A tennis ball! That would mean the world...*

Back in the examination room, the doctor showed her the scans, which clearly showed a red gummy bear lodged in the hollow under her arm. "My goodness," the doctor said, wide-eyed and chuckling with amazement. "I've only seen a handful of these in my career. What a treat! Something to show the kids, eh?" The woman didn't bother to explain she and her husband did not have children, and even if they did, these hypothetical offspring would have much preferred something green and buoyant, or at least something that didn't soften and melt under the scorching heat of the sun, turning into useless goo.

Making The Rounds

A pinecone floats through space, lost and alone. It goes over to Jupiter's house to say hello. Jupiter is away on business. The pinecone pops over to Mars to see if she has plans tonight, but Mars is burning with rage after an argument it had with Venus. It's clear to the pinecone the two planets need some time apart. The pinecone carries on, orbiting over Earth. Even though the pinecone has no memory of ever having been to Earth, there's always been a vague attraction to the luminescent planet. Earth and the pinecone have always seen each other as *just friends*, but now the pinecone wonders if there might be some potential for something more. The pinecone imagines their potential first date: the two of them picnicking on the banks of the Milky Way, then riding the Big Dipper together and throwing their heads back with pure pleasure and exhilaration. The pinecone is eager to ask out Earth, but, at the same time, it feels it has endured enough rejection for one trip. Perhaps it will try again the next time it's in the neighborhood. The pinecone doesn't want to appear desperate, after all.

All of this daydreaming has exhausted the pinecone. It decides to stop off at a motel on the moon. Through a shroud of hazy cumulus clouds, Earth flashes a little wink as the pinecone drifts on towards the VACANCY sign.

Elvis Dies

An Elvis impersonator had filled a page in a notebook with dirty jokes, so he went to an open mic comedy night to test them out. The open mic took place in a black box theater in the northern region of the city, edging on the suburbs. At the top of the show, the emcee explained the format of the evening. Three random audience members had been given buttons that connected to three red light bulbs on stage. If someone with a button didn't care for a certain comic's material, they were encouraged to press their button. A red light bulb represented a strike against the comic; if all three light bulbs lit up, the comic was done, sent back to the proverbial dugout without finishing their set. This made Elvis nervous. Sweat bled through his armpits, staining his white jumpsuit, which was lined with sequins around the lapels.

The first comic was a leaf of a young man. He wore thick glasses and skinny jeans. *This guy is cooked!* Elvis thought from his seat in the back of the room. But no. The little guy murdered, as they say in the business. *Beginner's luck,* Elvis thought. Another comic went up, this one a punk rock girl with one side of her head shaved, and she, too, left the crowd bent over in their chairs laughing. No bulbs. No strikes. *This crowd must be easy to please. Bodes well for me!* Elvis thought, giving himself a much-needed pep talk. His armpit stains were the size of the moon.

As the emcee called Elvis to the stage, the room filled with a scattered and somewhat skeptical round of applause. Elvis drew in a deep breath and strode up to the mic in four lunging steps. Immediately, the first light bulb flicked on, glowing red. Some in the crowd snickered. A bit of Elvis's confidence chipped away like flakes from a crumbling ember. He turned away from the daunting trio of bulbs, opened his notebook, and recited his first joke, which was about cunnilingus. Not even halfway through the joke, he saw a second red light pop up in his periphery. "Is it hot in here, or is it just me?" he asked the audience, flashing his iconic pearly whites. A pockmarked kid in the first row said, "Do you need medical attention?" A moment later, someone else chimed in: "Sing us a song!" Elvis opened his mouth, but it seemed he had forgotten to speak, let alone sing. The third light lit up, sealing his fate. The curtain was aflame with red.

The Sun and the Mooning

The Sun pulls down its shorts and moons the galaxy, eclipsing itself with its dark red behind. Earth is outraged and drafts a petition. Neptune and Saturn sign immediately, just happy to be included. Uranus refuses, and defiantly joins the Sun in mooning the other planets, a snotty little sibling emulating an older, brattier child. Mars, like Earth, is hot with indignation and organizes a protest rally. All told, Earth and Mars are the only picketers to show up — Jupiter is away on a work retreat, while Venus and Mercury are too nervous to show their support. The Sun knows where they live.

Surface Level

A cluttered brain opens the hatch of its owner's skull and takes a path down to a pond in a woodsy clearing. The afternoon is windy and overcast. The brain is swollen and aches from too many third shifts, too much overtime. It finds a bench and sits underneath the shade of a hawthorn tree and lights a cigarette. The brain ponders the ducks gliding effortlessly along the surface of the water, then exhales. A thought is embedded in the smoke — *don't forget to file your taxes*. The wind snatches away both the smoke and the thought. The brain takes another drag, exhales. Another thought floats off — *pay off student loans*. Inhale. Exhale. *Gotta call the realtor later*. Inhale. Exhale. *Quarterly reports due tomorrow*. Somewhere in the distance, porch chimes sing. The brain senses the hint of a familiar song, but doesn't investigate further.

Common Ground

I was driving down an unfamiliar road yesterday when I approached a house with a flag in the front yard that read *Re-Elect Rasputin For Mayor*. On impulse, I slowed and veered into the driveway. *Rasputin — what a clown!* I thought. My vision started to blur, I was so angry. I got out of my car and knocked firmly on the front door. A man wearing an Oxford button down shirt and khaki slacks answered. "Can I help you?" he said. I said, "Rasputin, eh? Haven't you had enough of his chicanery during his first term?" The old mystic had run for mayor several years ago, campaigning on a platform of mandatory self-flagellation in the workplace and sexual orgies in public parks. Many in town claimed they wanted a political outsider, a new perspective, and so he beat the incumbent mayor in a landslide. But soon, the town took on a dark mood. Crows circled around everywhere and heavy clouds crowded the sky, enclosing the town in a depressive bubble. This, on top of all his shady interpersonal dealings. "He accused my wife of trying to poison him with her award-winning blueberry pie," I told the man. The man shrugged and said, "He fixed the roads with a flick of his hand. Not a tax dollar spent." I retorted, "He bit off my parrot's head and drank its blood like a milkshake. This was on the same night he accused my wife of trying to poison him! We invited him over for dinner to congratulate him on his electoral triumph and he went ballistic." The man held up his hands and said, "He got rid of the dirty cops. Zapped them into pillars of salt with a single glare." Feeling my face grow hot, I said, "He organized a mass orgy — on Easter Sunday!" The man smiled. "I know! It was pretty fun." He had a point there. I said, "It was! The pigs in a blanket were a nice touch." I tipped my hat and got back in my car and continued on to my destination. I still haven't changed my mind about that Rasputin fellow, but I can hardly wait until the next orgy. I have a feeling it will be even better than the first.

The Physical

A man was asked by his doctor if he was single, widowed, or married. The man said, "My dentist is my spouse." The doctor ticked off the appropriate box which corresponded to the man's answer. "Do you have any children?" the doctor asked. The man said, "My teeth are my children." The doctor said, "How wonderful. Can I meet them?" The man said, "Of course, but they are a bit shy. And one of my canines recently moved away for college." The doctor nodded sympathetically. The doctor's children were not teeth, but pubic hairs. They had been away to college years ago, and had since returned to the doctor's home, and had started to crimp and gray a little at the ends. Not one of them ever bothered to get jobs or find a suitable partner and reproduce children of their own. Coming back home was their version of settling down. The doctor had to admit, it was a little sad to see the children grow old without realizing their full potential, out in the broader world. "Ah well," the doctor said. "We were young once, too, weren't we?" He then asked the man to open wide so he could say hello to the little ones.

Elvis's Homecoming

An Elvis impersonator returned home for Thanksgiving dinner.
His mother, a Marilyn Monroe impersonator, greeted him at the
front door wearing a white dress and a wig full of shimmering
blond curls. Elvis blushed as his eyes accidentally passed over her
blossoming dress, upturned by a gust of air coming from a floor
grate in the entryway. "Oh, mom," Elvis said, shielding his eyes. He
stepped inside and waved to his father, sitting in the living room
dressed in a constricting black jacket and baggy tweed trousers, a
bowler hat cocked on the crown of his head. "How are things,
pop?" His father, a Charlie Chaplin impersonator, indifferently
seesawed his stout mustache, his attention glued to the football
game on TV. He stabbed a fork into a leather shoe on a TV dinner
tray and sucked the shoelace into his mouth as if it was a thick
noodle. Suddenly, the sound of someone beatboxing came from the
kitchen, and a man moonwalked into the living room, wearing a
military jacket and a single white polyester glove with starry
sequins. Elvis hugged his brother, a Michael Jackson
impersonator, who was followed by his wife, a big-haired, fast-
talking Dolly Parton impersonator, and their two boys: one slim
and poised, the other husky and frantically waving his arms. Like
Charlie Chaplin, they, too, wore bowler hats. The boys pinched
each other and bonked one another on the head; Dolly Parton
snapped at the pint-sized Laurel and Hardy, demanding they cool
it if they knew what was good for them. "Starting them early, I see,"
Elvis commented. His brother squeezed Hardy's shoulder proudly
and said, "I was thinking we could bring them to the state fair like
dad did with us." Charlie Chaplin swung his cane, signaling to his
sons that they were blocking the television, as the lip of the shoe
flopped out of his mouth. When it was time to say grace, everyone
held hands around the dinner table filled with food, and Marilyn
Monroe sang a sultry rendition of "Happy Birthday," just as she did
every year. Charlie Chaplin did a softshoe as he carved the turkey,
and Elvis's mouth watered as he daydreamed of funnel cakes and
corn dogs.

Open Dialogue

The refrigerator coos. The freezer mews. The oven purrs. The microwave moos. The toaster buzzes. The air fryer sings. The dishwasher gibbers. The washing machine wails. The dryer howls. The coffee machine snorts. The vacuum yowls. The blender roars. The food processor screeches. The slow cooker grunts. The rice cooker hisses. The juicer neighs. The waffle iron whinnies. The coffee grinder gobbles. The deep fryer nickers. The garbage disposal growls. The water purifier whispers. The sewing machine warbles. The ceiling fan pants. The humidifier bellows. The dehumidifier hums. The water heater farts. The domestic robot does the same.

Floating Grounds

Ghost was having an out of body experience. This had never happened before. Ghost hovered over his translucent form as it slept in his tiny twin bed. As he studied himself, Ghost realized then his ghostly self was actually pretty handsome. Perhaps he should put himself out there a bit more, strike up more conversations with the neighborhood pinecones and flower beds. Eventually, Ghost grew a bit bored of watching himself sleeping peacefully, not budging at all. He scratched at the glow-in-the-dark stars on the ceiling. He rearranged the books and pens on the desk in the corner. Then, out of nowhere, another ghost flew in through the window. The ghost looked at Ghost confused. Ghost said, "Who are you?" The stranger ghost said, "I'm your ghost. Well, I was." Ghost said, "When was this?" The stranger ghost said, "When before you were Ghost and just Body. I had your job before you did. Every entity, living or deceased, must have a ghost. If you are sentient, you are haunted." Ghost said, "So I took your job?" The stranger ghost shrugged. "No hard feelings. I moonlight at a library now. Just wanted to check out the old stomping grounds." Ghost felt sad for the ghost he had put out of work, hoping the same thing would not happen to him.

Miss Lacy

When I got out of the pool, I noticed the tattoo on my bicep had shrunk. I have many tattoos, mostly of faded pinup girls, but this one is different: a brown and black heart branded with the name of my first dog, Miss Lacy. A beagle. We got her from the local dairy farm. I named her after my kindergarten teacher, who had a tender nature and soulful brown eyes, and who encouraged my interest in reading hefty encyclopedias and ventriloquism. Though my interests have shifted since then, the tattoo will be with me forever.

As I toweled off, I told myself the tattoo would grow back to its normal size over time. Everything would be fine. I warned my daughter not to dive so close to the shallow end.

Elvis Remembers

After Joe Brainard

An Elvis impersonator was walking his dog, Boswell, when he suddenly felt nostalgic about his childhood. It was early spring and the weather was warming. The sky was clear and blue all around, and the trees had just exploded with colorful leaves. Elvis remembered about how, as a child, he was vaguely aroused by the fishy smell from the Bradford pear trees that presently surrounded him. He remembered wearing corduroy pants for Thanksgiving dinner. He remembered storytime in the library, and getting to pick out a book afterward. He remembered that some books had brown smudges on the pages — from chocolate candy, best case scenario. The pages were yellow and stiff but well-loved. He remembered his first dog, Mary, whom his mother had named after Mary Tyler Moore. Mary had felt like a little sister to Elvis. That, or maybe Elvis felt more akin to a dog. In any case, their bond was strong. He remembered taking Mary to an empty football field on Sunday mornings, throwing a frisbee, and watching her chase after it and bring it back in a matter of seconds. No matter how many times he threw the thing, she never seemed to get tired. For Elvis, this was his idea of heaven.

The Easter Ghost

A ghost was trying to lay eggs in time for Easter. The ghost had been trying diligently since Saint Patrick's Day, taking supplements, trying to get a good night's rest every night, no smoking or drinking. Every morning the ghost would sit at a grassy patch beneath the same sycamore tree in the meadow and wait for something to happen. Occasionally, an acorn would fall from the tree, traveling right through the ghost and bouncing once or twice before settling on the ground beside it. Beyond this, not much happened. The ghost looked out at the other sycamores. The early spring breeze traversed through their leaves, turning them over gently, like a baker gracefully kneading dough. The ghost tried to remember about its life before it was a ghost, but it could barely remember the day before, let alone a previous lifetime. With no results a few days before Easter Sunday, the ghost was feeling discouraged and hopeless. The ghost decided to go to the convenience store in town and pick up a pack of cigarettes and a bottle of Jameson. The ghost sat on the sidewalk outside the store, smoking and getting drunk. Halfway through the bottle, the ghost suddenly felt a rumble in its midsection, as if something was doing cartwheels in its belly. The ghost rushed to the meadow, towards the tree with the luscious grassy patch. A few yards away, the rumble grew into a more chaotic, forceful feeling. The ghost halted, lowering itself to the ground. Something fell. The ghost looked down. It was a stone, a big one, round and smooth.

Process

A poet is giving birth to a novel. She is very displeased to be bringing a novel into the world, but she has little choice, since she has an agreement with her publisher. The contractions are painful — the feeling is sharp, blinding, all-consuming. She didn't have nearly as much trouble when birthing her previous two collections of light verse. She is sweating and hysterical. This feels like more than one book. Perhaps there's a sequel inside her as well? A trilogy? Goodness, how is she going to manage the publicity, the signing lines, the film adaptations? This is more than what she ever bargained for. The nurse offers her hand and instructs the poet to breathe, her voice like aloe vera. Outside the hospital window, the weather is dark and stormy. Trees whip violently in the wind as lightning flashes closeby. In the distance, an old country manor sits atop a hill. No lights, not even a single candle, illuminates the shadowy windows. A feeling of dread fills the poet. The doctor raises his head to announce it won't be much longer now: he can see the deckled edges. The poet clamps her eyes shut. She's yearning for some sort of denouement, some tidy conclusion, but little does she know this is only the rising action, and this conflict refuses to fit tidily into couplets, or even a sonnet.

Elvis on the Corner

An Elvis impersonator took a job spinning a sign for a textbook store. The job paid eight dollars an hour. It wasn't ideal, but in between gigs there were worse ways to find money. Elvis was stationed on a busy intersection across from the university. Since the textbook store was an off-site store, Elvis was not allowed to spin his sign on campus, which was populated with verdant trees and peaceful gazebos. The heat from the sun was oppressive. The humidity was off the charts. Pit stains formed underneath Elvis's silk jumpsuit in mere minutes. No matter. Elvis popped in his ear buds and switched his iPod on shuffle. The first song to come up was "Gimme! Gimme! Gimme! (A Man After Midnight)" by ABBA. This wasn't Elvis's favorite song, but he went with the flow, pumping his knees and pointing dramatically at soccer moms in their air-conditioned minivans. Balding men in convertibles and freight truckers shot Elvis screwy looks, as if he represented everything vile and immoral and distasteful about the world. Elvis's vision blurred. His brain boiled over and his consciousness seemed to bubble and melt like lava. He felt he had no control over his body and he didn't care. He felt he was a wild flame dancing in the heart of a raging, ravenous fire. The pit stains continued to grow, until the entire jumpsuit was dark with sweat. The song faded. Elvis slowed a little to catch his breath. The light at the intersection changed from green to yellow, then from yellow to red. The next song started as the light turned green again and Elvis found a new groove, this time to Black Sabbath.

The Cavity

My wife and I have spent our entire lives inside the chest cavity of an old man. We don't have a house here, just a small living space on top of the gallbladder. We are very small and don't require much room, anyway. We are middle-aged, and still, it's unclear to us, were we placed here, together, so long ago we can't remember? Or were we born into being inside this human, from the very beginning? We discuss these questions only occasionally, over dandelion tea or a game of Rummikub. Candles light our days and nights, though there is very little difference for us. A rumbling of acid reflux from the esophagus typically signals a reaction to a heavy dinner, and with that, the end of the day. The meaty heart above serves as both our sun and moon. There are no stars to speak of, metaphorical or otherwise.

Just a Few Questions

A few seconds after the black SUV pulled into my driveway, a short woman stepped out and knocked on my front door. She wore a gray pantsuit and wielded a clipboard. My dog barked viciously, as she always does. I didn't bother to calm her down as I opened the door and said, "Can I help you?" The woman said, "Yes, I'm looking for Wayne Daniel Heely." "She doesn't live here anymore," I said. "She?" the woman said. "Sorry, I meant *he* no longer lives here. I just moved in and am still getting his mail. For some reason, when I skim over the name I see 'Wanda,' at first glance, not Wayne." The woman scribbled on her clipboard, not looking at me. She said, "I see. Old residence." "What do you need him for?" I asked. "I have some questions for him," the woman said. "I'd be happy to try answering them," I said. The woman said, "I'm not sure you'd understand the context behind most of these inquiries." My dog licked my fingers. I said, "Try me." She flipped over the top page on the clipboard and said, "In which state do you intend to pass away?" "Wyoming would be my first choice," I said, "but I'd also settle for Idaho or Montana." The woman said, "Are you familiar with the plays of Molière? If so, do you have a favorite?" I answered, "I am very familiar with Molière. I wrote my Master's thesis on *The Imaginary Invalid*, which Molière labelled a *comédie-ballet*. It was also his final play. That would be my favorite, I'd say." The woman said, "Have you ever tried on a pair of female undergarments?" "Yes, my mother dressed me up as a girl until I was eleven years old," I said. "Are you Jewish or Italian?" the woman said. "Neither," I said, "but I get mistaken for being Jewish even by Jewish people." The woman said, "Have you ever coordinated an assassination attempt?" "No comment," I said. The woman said, "Have you ever maintained a garden?" "No," I said, "now get off my property." "Thanks for your time; we'll let you know the results in three to five business days," the woman said. She then walked back to her SUV and drove away, and I wondered how Wayne could have answered her questions any more perfectly than I had.

Champ

I was petting my dog Champ when his head suddenly fell off and landed in my lap. I screamed and bolted upright. Champ's head bounced onto the floor, as did his fluffy ten pound body. Weeping, I picked up the parts of my decapitated dog and realized he was stuffed with cotton. His eyes were made of glass. His floppy pink tongue was felt fabric. I had taken care of him for seven years and never noticed any of this. Had he always been this way, or had his body suddenly taken this plushy form as a result of his spontaneous death? Feelings of shame and remorse worked through me. My poor Champ. How could I have let this happen?

I checked my goldfish to be sure they had not faced a similar fate, then I curled up in bed and cried myself into a fitful sleep. When I awoke it was late afternoon. The sun was just beginning to lower behind the trees. I opened a window and heard a group of kids playing basketball in the street. It was a Saturday. A breeze worked its way around the edges of the room, moving like secret whispers. It was not too late to start digging. It was not too late to go for a walk, either. I couldn't make up my mind, so I grabbed my shovel and started to stroll.

Elvis and Tiny Tim

An Elvis impersonator decided to visit the crypt of Tiny Tim. Elvis
and Tiny Tim had been dear friends when Tiny was alive and
kicking. They worked the same rooms and stayed in the same
hotels in Las Vegas, the Catskills, and Miami. Whenever they
would bump into each other Elvis would be starstruck and Tiny
would offer to buy him a drink. Hunched over the end of a
cavernous hotel bar, the two of them would talk about the tiresome
routine of the road, their aspirations, the women they'd left behind.
Tiny claimed to be in his late thirties, but Elvis knew he was
fibbing. There were the deep wrinkles, of course, and the tired,
world-weary eyes, but the most telling thing was Tiny's wisdom,
which was on par with that of a white-haired sage. For Elvis,
meeting Tiny Tim was the most meaningful connection he'd ever
made in his early nomadic years. He missed Tiny dearly, but it took
decades for him to make the trip to pay his respects.

Elvis placed a bouquet of purple tulips outside of Tiny's marble
crypt, in a well-lit mausoleum somewhere in the Midwest. He
closed his eyes and made the sign of the cross. He kept his eyes
closed for an extra few seconds, thinking of a piece of advice Tiny
had shared decades ago. *"Life is a brief spark from a flint. You can
either nurture the spark into a flame, which can grow into a
beautiful warming fire, or you can let it fizzle out. Poof. Nothing.
You've got what it takes to set this world on fire, kid. Just tend to
the flame."* Elvis imagined Tiny said this to a multitude of aspiring
performers he met over the years; still, his words made an indelible
impression on the young Elvis. He had never forgotten Tiny's
sentiment, and had done his best to live up to its meaning.
Eventually, Elvis opened his eyes. He had no idea how much time
had passed. The tulips seemed to be a shade lighter, but Elvis
couldn't be sure. Tiny always liked to play tricks with the light.

Surprise Guests

It was mid-afternoon, and I decided to take a nap on the couch. I had not slept well the night before: my dreams had been populated by eerie hospitals, ghostly cemeteries, and stormy skies. The nap turned out to be much longer than I anticipated, almost two hours. When I awoke, the sun was draining away like bath water through the trees. Something was bothering me. My right ear felt clogged, as if a thimbleful of molasses was trapped inside it. A low hum reverberated through my ear canal. I had not gone swimming recently, and I was good about keeping my head away from the shower's stream. Maybe I had slept on my right side in a funny position, but otherwise I could not explain the odd feeling. I was stumped. Still, I sat thinking about it. Harriet, my beagle, barked at something outside. Her sound was muffled, as if she was barking through a pillow. It was almost totally dark outside. I got up, went to the kitchen, and tossed some bacon on the frying pan. In another pan, I cracked a couple eggs and let them cook on low heat.

The deep hum in my ear changed in pitch, going higher and higher until it sounded like a soprano hitting their final note. I winced as I reached for the medicine cabinet. Harriet was going nuts, running circles around the front door. I flipped over the bacon then went to see what was outside. In the pitch black of night, I saw nothing but the shadows of trees and the flurries of moths. I was about to close the door when I heard a miniscule voice say, "Hello!" I looked down. On my welcome mat stood four tiny people, each no bigger than a board game piece. I felt a shift in the pressure in my head, as if something was crawling out of my ear canal. Just then, another high-pitched voice came from my ear. "Hello, comrades! So good to see you again!" I rushed to the nearest mirror and saw a tiny man clutching to my outer ear. He wore green suspenders and was even smaller than his token-sized friends. I said, "Who are you?" The tiny man said, "I'm Gerald. I just had a fantastic nap inside your ear canal. Much obliged!" I said, "This is a dream. It has to be." "Haven't you heard of our kind before?" Gerald said, "We're making our annual migration to South America." The tiny people at the door said, "May we come in? Something smells delicious." Before I could answer they were already helping each other take off their coats.

Early Retirement

An actor in a play cries, "I've had ENOUGH!" and storms off stage mid-scene. The actor leaves the theater. The other actors follow the departing actor and the audience follows the other actors into the town square. The initial departing actor starts on the walk home. It takes him some time to realize he is being followed. "Why are you following me?" he says over his shoulder to the crowd on the sidewalk. The woman who plays the departing actor's wife responds by reciting the next line in the play. The departing actor says, "I'm moving on from this whole mess. Have my understudy play my part. Just leave me alone, please." He continues on his way home, and the other actors and audience members continue to follow. The other actors recite their scripted lines and blocking, despite the actor not participating. The show goes on through the town square, over the railroad tracks, onward to the outskirts of town. The audience members laugh and gasp at the appropriate parts, nudging each other with enjoyment. The sun grows heavy in the sky. Invisible insects begin their throbbing nighttime songs in the brush, an earthy Greek chorus. Finally, the departing actor arrives home. He goes inside without a word, no curtain call or encore. The crowd enters behind him. Not bothering to brush his teeth or take off his clothes, the departing actor falls hard onto the bed. His bedroom is crowded with actors and audience members staring down at him. Everyone is antsy for intermission. The play is almost over, but it still feels like an eternity. The departing actor ignores everyone and stares out the window, at the moon hanging in the sky like a marquee sign.

Dear Elvis...

An Elvis impersonator was reading his fan mail, which he received every Saturday in a large canvas sack that arrived on his doorstep. The vast majority of the letters were written by audience members from recent shows, who were either extremely touched or extremely displeased by the performance. *I saw you perform at the Oak Grove Retirement Home last week, and just wanted to let you know you did my soul good that day.... Or, I caught your act at the Gondolier's Pizza Parlor a few days ago, and let me tell you, you don't know the first thing about Elvis. I saw The King at the Las Vegas Hilton in 1975. Boy, was he a sight. He did three HOUR LONG encores. A sweating, howling messiah, he was. A saint among mortals. Buddy, you've got a long way to go to do him justice....* Elvis had to laugh at letters like this. If only the author knew what he knew, that Elvis was more than just a dancing monkey to be gawked at. Elvis was and is a philosophy, a way of living life. Everyone has a little Elvis inside them, waiting to be unleashed to the world. Everyone knows how to transform joy into a hip shake, how to hitch their lip in a sensual smile, how to brighten their hooded eyes into dazzling diamonds. Everyone can kung fu kick to their heart's content. There's just something holding most people back.

Elvis smiled and shook his head as he set aside the letter. He plucked a glossy 8x10 from a pile of headshots and signed it. Good or bad, nasty or nice, everyone received a headshot, inscribed with a silver fine-point tip marker. *Vegas '75...* Elvis thought as he autographed the photo. *What a year...*

The New System

I walked into a building I thought was the library, but it turned out to be the courthouse. A row of stern middle-aged women sat behind bulletproof glass windows. Distraught families occupied benches, holding each other and crying as men and women in flashy suits walked in and out of court rooms. Confused, I approached a security guard standing by a walk-through metal detector and said, "Excuse me, but I thought this was the library. I have some books to return." The guard said, "You can bring that up to the judge. Empty your pockets." The guard held out a plastic bowl; I put in my wallet and keys. "What should I do with these?" I said, holding up my books by Colette and Voltaire. The guard called over another guard, who held a German Shepherd by a leash. The guard opened the books and the dog sniffed the words with a clinical, suspicious stare. The second guard shook his head and hauled off the books without a word. I said, "Hey, I need to return those to the library." The guard said, "First they will be processed as evidence. We have a new system." He gestured for me to walk through the metal detector. Once I was on the other side, he told me to put my hands behind my back. He put me in handcuffs. "I've committed no crime," I said as he recited my rights. At the far end of the lobby, by the restrooms, I saw my mother weeping alone on a bench. When she saw me, she rushed over. "Oh, darling, it's so unjust what they are putting you through. We will fight until the truth is heard," she said as she fought back tears. "Ma, what the hell is happening?" I said. She said, "I'm not sure. I just received a letter telling me to be here." "Keep your voices down," the guard said.

Shelley's Realization

I took my regular stool at Roscoe's Tavern and looked to see if any of my friends were around. A gray-haired couple around my age sat a couple stools down from me on one side. On my other side, sitting by the wall was a young man in a weathered overcoat that seemed to be from a different era. I didn't recognize anyone in the bar except for Tonya, the barkeep. Without having to ask, she brought me a bourbon with a splash of water. The mysterious young man at the bar was staring at me. Over the years, I've learned it's best to confront these sorts of people head-on. I said, "Can I help you, buddy?" "Perhaps you can," said the young man, "my name is Percy Bysshe Shelley. I'm afraid I'm a bit lost." "Shelley, the Romantic poet?" I said. "I've penned a few poems, yes, as well as some tracts on atheism. You're familiar with my work?" Shelley said. I said, "I wouldn't say familiar, but I remember reading 'Ode To The West Wind' in grammar school. Say, if you're really Shelley, you should be able to recite some of it for us." Shelley said, "Forgive me, but I can recall very little at this juncture. My countrymen and I were caught in a treacherous storm while sailing. I was cast from the ship and hit my head on a rock. That's the last thing I remember before I awoke here. Tell me, sir, are we in the Kingdom of Sardinia?" "Sardinia," I said, "Is that in Idaho?" "Nevermind," Shelley said, then turned to Tonya. "May I borrow some parchment and a quill? I must write Mary post haste." Tonya tore off a stretch of paper from the receipt machine and handed Shelley a pen with the name of a cheap motel on it. "You'll need a couple stamps if it's going overseas," she said, "all we got's those five cent ones. Unfortunately, I don't think those will get you far." Shelley's face changed, and it was then he seemed to realize he was nowhere near the Kingdom of Sardinia. Tonya poured Shelley a shot and said, "On the house, sugar." An old Patsy Cline song came on the jukebox. "Is that my mother?" Shelley said. No one said anything, but for a fleeting moment I'd had the same thought.

Your New Liver

A delivery man knocked on my door. When I answered, he said,
"Your new liver has arrived. I just need you to provide your John
Hancock here." He held a clipboard and pen. A small blue cooler
sat by his feet. I said, "You must have the wrong house. My liver
has worked like a charm my entire life. Actually, we have cultivated
a very copasetic relationship. My liver takes care of the bills, and I
do the grocery shopping. If anything needs to be repaired around
the house, say the electrical panel needs to be rewired, I'm the guy.
However, on nights when I can't sleep, my liver lets me cry on its
shoulder, and it will even read me the complete works of
Montaigne, if I ask it to. My liver is my rock, my lifeline." "I'm glad
for you," the delivery man said, "but I assume you haven't been
keeping up with the news. The law now requires you to receive a
new liver every two years." "I assure you I have no complaints with
my original liver, and there must be plenty of people out there who
have faulty livers and are in much more dire need. Giving it to me
would be a waste of a liver," I said. The delivery man said, "This
liver has all the necessary updates. It's up to legal code. The liver
you have currently would not pass annual inspection, which can
lead to fines and possible prison time." "Annual inspection?" I said,
befuddled. "Lift your shirt," the delivery man said, raising his pen,
which wasn't a pen at all, but a scalpel. "Wait," I said, "let me grab
a pen. I have a whole collection."

My Biographer

I was downtown, walking to the pharmacy to pick up some prescriptions when I noticed a little girl on a scooter trailing me. My eyes met hers, and she stared at me with a mixture of interest and something else. I couldn't be sure if she was repulsed by me, or just intrigued. "Can I help you?" I said. "Don't mind me," she said, "I'm only your biographer." I said, "My biographer? Who would ever want to read a book about me?" The little girl said, "Plenty of people. You've had a long and storied career." "I've worked in a fruitcake factory for thirty years. I've seen one or two workers get their arm stuck in a machine, but nothing more exciting than that," I said. The little girl blinked. I added, "Would you like to know where I was born and who my parents were?" "Oh, I have all the relevant ancestral information I need. However, there was the time you tried to form a labor union," the girl said, "can you tell me more about that?" She took out a small notepad and pencil from her gingham dress. "How old are you?" I said. "Answer my question first," she said. The colors in the sky above the courthouse started to change rapidly, from calming hues of blue to vibrant orange to fearsome crimson. The temperature plummeted. Leaves snapped off of trees and fell into tidy, self-contained piles until a treacherous wind blew them away. Shopkeepers brought in their sale carts and pedestrians rushed into nearby buildings, but the girl remained stoic behind her notepad and scooter. Shouting over the wind, I said, "The labor union failed because Howard Lentil, my co-leader, wanted different things than I wanted. He wanted two-hour lunch breaks and three weeks off *during December* — our busiest time of the year. That's not going to fly at a fruitcake factory!" As dark clouds began to swell in the sky, the little girl began taking notes. She said, "Lentil, Lentil... spelled like the legume?"

Sex and the Opera

A woman wants sex. Her husband says, "But we have tickets to the opera." The woman says, "I don't care. It's been so long. I'm about to burst." Her husband says, "We have plenty of sex. It's in the cupboards, in the refrigerator, in every drawer and closet of every room. But tonight we're going to the opera. These tickets cost me a third of my paycheck." The woman says, "Can't we order in some opera tonight? All I can think about is sex and I don't feel like leaving the house." The husband waves the tickets and says, "But these seats are right behind the orchestra pit." "Ugh," says the woman, "I hate that section. Remember how the tuba blocked my view last time?" The husband sighs and complies, before the spat turns into a bigger argument. He picks up the phone. The woman goes over to the pantry and opens up a container of sex. It smells sour and musty. She checks the expiration date; surprisingly, it's still good. Using a plastic baby spoon, the woman takes a small bite of sex. The taste is the same as ever: simultaneously comforting and disappointing, with a slight aftertaste of guilt. The husband hangs up and says, "They will deliver the opera singers in half an hour. I also ordered a side of garlic knots." He looks at his wife with her stacked containers of sex. Taking off his shoes and socks, he says, "Well, hell. I might as well have some, too."

Pappy

It was a dour, overcast day. Everything was made bloated and sad-looking by the morning's gray rain. I was sitting at my desk by the window, balancing my checkbook, when I saw a man stumbling up the cul-de-sac, moving towards my house. His suit was wrinkled and torn. It looked as if animals had attacked him. As he approached, I realized that the man was my grandfather, who we had just buried four days earlier. He staggered up the front steps and let himself in. "I forgot my pager," Pappy said with an agitated wave. He went into his old room and I heard him rummaging around in the drawers. I said, "Please keep it down, the baby is sleeping." For whatever reason, Pappy became more irritated and the noise of his rooting around grew even louder. I got up to see what was the matter. A mountain of shirts and underwear sat atop the bed. Drawers were scattered on the bedroom floor. The room had been a mess when Pappy was around, and now it was my designated dump-site in the house, I hate to admit. The maggots in Pappy's forehead were having a feast; I could see parts of his moon white skull. He said, "I'll be damned. You people! I'm still warm in my grave and you start moving my stuff around. Hell, I bet you already gave away my pager to the Salvation Army!" I said, "We haven't left the house since the funeral. What do you need a pager for in heaven, anyway? You can't take it with you." "First of all, we don't call it heaven. You don't know the first thing about what goes on there. Second, I've been making contacts. Big names. I have some very exciting projects on the horizon. I need to be accessible at all times," he said. He kicked over a pile of old polyester ties, which unearthed my old Hit Clips player. His milky eyes expanded. He snatched up the toy and exclaimed "Thank Christ!" As he hurried out of the house, he said, "Big things are happening. Large things. You'll see. Very soon, you'll see." The rain was letting up. He marched on to eternity.

Disobedience

My ventriloquist dummy has been very disobedient lately. I say, "Clean your room," and all he does is sit at his desk, staring blankly out the window. I tell him, "Help me bring in the groceries, please," and he remains on the couch, his wooden face glued to the TV. "Eat your brussel sprouts," I advise at the kitchen table; in response, he slumps in his chair like a dead man. "Fine," I conclude, "go to bed hungry for all I care." My dummy slouches further, falling onto the floor in a lifeless heap. I drop the dishes in the sink and turn off the lights, but he doesn't get up. When he was small, he was afraid of the dark, but no longer. No one ever told me this would be so difficult.

The Broken Toothpick

I killed a cockroach last night. I was reading Samuel Beckett when I noticed it hobbling toward me, like an old dog wanting to play fetch. My dirty old shoe took care of that dirty old dog. I pancaked it into the hardwood, then clawed it up with an old get well soon card and dropped it unceremoniously in the trash bin. When I came back to the couch, I noticed a prickly brown leg on the floor, by my glass of bourbon. The leg was bent at the middle: a broken toothpick stripped of its garnish. I wondered if I would have minded if it had fallen into my drink. I wondered if I would have liked the phantom flavor it had to offer.

Uptown Girl

At daybreak, I awoke with a start. It felt as though gears were grinding and shifting in my chest, moving around like a Rubik's Cube. A wobbly baritone hum started on my left side, then reverberated through my entire body. I thought I was having a heart attack. I was about to ask my heart what was going on when it started singing the opening notes of "Uptown Girl," by Billy Joel. With every rising note, the clouds parted little by little, like set pieces. It wasn't the most polished performance, but I was still impressed. "I had no idea you could sing like that," I told my heart. "Thank you," my heart said, "I've been taking lessons from my neighbor, the lungs. I'm still working on my pitch, but it means a lot for you to say that." We got out of bed, my heart and I, and started the day. The sunlight slanting through the windows seemed to nourish us in new and transcendent ways.

Trick-or-Treat

I had the feeling my face was maybe a mask, so I grabbed a pillow case and went out trick-or-treating. I knocked on my neighbor Hank's door, eager for candy. "Trick-or-treat," I said when Hank answered. "Jeff, what the hell," Hank said, "it's nine o'clock on a Tuesday morning. Shouldn't you be at work?" I said, "I've just come to the realization I can't be completely certain my face is not a mask. In fact, I'm pretty sure my face *is* a mask. So I thought I'd make the most of the situation." Hank said, "Well, okay. Where's your costume?" "I've come to the realization I can't be entirely assured my clothes don't already make up a costume. Do you like it? Is it scary enough?" Hank said, "Not really. You're wearing that starched yellow shirt that always looks like it's about to snap in two. Not to mention those candy cane suspenders and gigantic shoes you're always tripping over. All you're missing is a bag of tricks and some clown make-up. Then you'd be ready to join the circus." "You know, it's funny you mention that. Because I've just come to the realization I can't be entirely certain...."

A Christian Burial

The lightbulb of the lamp on my desk flickered, then went out. The way it flickered wasn't spastic or random, though. It seemed the bulb was trying to telegraph a message; there was a sense of urgency behind the stark intervals of darkness, then light, darkness, light, brightening light, fading light, then permanent darkness. I unscrewed the defunct bulb and held it in my palm as if it was a communion wafer. Just then, I heard a warbling voice say, "Oh, blessed be! You received my message." "Come again?" I said, somewhat spooked. "I sent out a message in my dying moments and you saw it!" the bulb said. "Can you help me?" "I saw the flickering," I said, "but I don't know what it meant. How can I help?" The bulb said, "All I want is a proper Christian burial, with my kinfolk." I said, "You want me to dig a hole outside and put you in it?" "Yes. The family plot isn't far from here. I'll show you the way." I gently placed the bulb in the small front pocket of my backpack, where it would be safe and snug. Outside, the sun had gone away, but it wasn't completely dark yet. The sky was bruised with purple and gray. It reminded me of the countless black eyes I'd been dealt as a child.

I took my bicycle out of the shed behind the brick apartment complex where I live. The bulb said, "Make a left then turn right onto Thomas Street." As we rode, the wind whistled lightly, threading through my hair, and I felt like a bird, or a small aircraft, one of those early ones that didn't get too far off the ground. We rode over some railroad tracks on the edge of town. The road we were on turned into a dead end that fed into a park. I got off my bike and the bulb instructed me to go to the community garden. It was fully night now. Only a sliver of moon was pinned in the sky, but the stars shined more brightly than I had ever seen. Fireflies surrounded us like a battalion of benevolent little lanterns. Even without the light of the moon, I could have seen clearly in the dark. The fireflies journeyed with us as we followed the path to the garden.

I took the bulb out of the pouch on my backpack and walked it to the eastward edge of the garden. I dug a hole using a spade someone had left behind, then placed the gray bulb in the small hole. I piled the dirt back on then stood and stared at the mound of dirt. I recited a quote from one of my favorite movies, a buddy film from the 90s. Even though I hadn't known the bulb for long, I imagined it would appreciate the offbeat adieu. As I walked back to my bike, I noticed a woman around my age walking towards me. We didn't say a word as we passed each other, but still gave each other a polite, if not slightly fatigued, nod. I was able to see she had the same backpack as me, thanks to fireflies guiding her way.

Off-hours

Upon arriving home, a man takes off his hat, and in doing so, takes off his head as well. The man, however, does not notice this; he is exhausted after a long day at the office. He rests his head and hat on the table in the foyer. His headless body enters the dining room and sits down to dinner with his family. "How was everyone's day?" the head says from the other room. "Fine," says the man's wife, not noticing, her thoughts swirling in her wine glass. "Okay," say the two children, each of them looking at something shiny in their laps. "Pork chops. My favorite!" the head exclaims, smelling dinner on the table, then promptly falls asleep underneath the shade of the hat's brim.

Caring for the Children

My desk was becoming overpopulated with clutter; I felt it was time for some evictions. I first approached the pile of postcards I'd received months ago, from various friends on summer vacation. "It looks like you're behind on your rent," I said to the postcards. "You must pay today or I will begin the removal process." Quivering, the postcards said, "We're having trouble paying since the rent went up two months ago. We're sorry, but all the money we make goes to caring for our children." I said, "Where are your children? I see no children." "The stamps are our children," the postcards explained, "see, they are latched onto our breasts." "Alright, I'll give you two days to come up with the money. But no later." "But we are in between jobs…" the postcards looked like they wanted to give themselves papercuts. "Last extension!" I said, then moved onto the slim volumes of poetry, with their little tike bookmarks nestled in between their endearingly weathered paperback covers.

Artaud's Ghost

There was a frantic knock on my door. I answered, and was met with the ghost of Antonin Artaud. The ghost was of Artaud as a child. He had thin lips and piercing charcoal-colored eyes. He held a grenade in both hands as if it were a dead bird. "Come out to play, please," Artaud said in French. "I'm afraid I'm busy," I replied, also in French, "I'm up to my eyeballs in ungraded essays." Artaud said, "But I've just come up with a game. It's called 'All Writing Is Pigshit.'" I said, "Oh, is it anything like Twister?" "No," Artaud said, "however, it is very similar to other games I've invented. In fact, it's essentially identical to my most famous parlor game, 'Revolt Against Poetry.' I simply transposed the rules word-for-word and gave it a new title." I had zoned out for a moment. My thoughts stumbled back to this time when I myself was a child and my father had given me a snowglobe as a souvenir from a business trip. I remembered the tiny, bundled-up pedestrians frozen on the sidewalk of the ceramic sculpture inside the glass and the giant knife-like skyscrapers, stoic and unwavering against the torrent of glimmering snow. Vivid as this was in my memory, I couldn't remember what city the snowglobe depicted. It bugged me. Was it Baltimore? Boston? Philadelphia? Paris? After a beat, I snapped out of it and said, "Can I see that grenade?" "Certainly," Artaud said. "Pull the pin and the game will begin."

Executive Branch

My wife, Darla, did the sweetest thing for my birthday. After I got off work, she told me to put on my best suit and tie. I went upstairs to our bedroom, thinking, "Oh goody, we must be going out for a steak dinner." While she dressed in the master bedroom, I ducked into the guest room and I scrambled into my reliable sharkskin suit. I hadn't worn it in years but it still fit like a fish tank. While doing my Windsor my mouth watered as I envisioned a plate of flavorful au gratin potatoes, creamy macaroni and cheese, heavenly filet minion. I finished dressing, combed my hair, slapped on some aftershave, then raced downstairs. There, sitting in my living room with Darla, were three men in black suits and sunglasses with wires feeding into their ears. Darla was decked out in a regal evening gown. She wore a pearl necklace and held a designer clutch purse. "Good evening, Mr. President," said Darla, with a little curtsy that made me blush. I said, "What's going on? Who are these men?" Darla said, "You have a speech in one hour, Mr. President. This is your security detail." The three men were cutting their shaded eyes in different directions and murmuring phrases like "Cathead has arrived," and "Are things ready at Omelette City?" into their discreet communication devices. Outside our front door, a sea of protesters holding signs rallied and chanted. "I thought we were having a steak dinner," I said. "Did the reservations fall through?" One of the men approached me and said, "The motorcade is ready, Mr. President. We must be swift. The police can hold off the protestors for so long." I didn't like his tone. I snapped. "Listen, buddy, I call the shots around here. I'm the president. The next time you pop off to me, it'll be your head." The guard said nothing, but I saw his face swell with redness. Another guard stepped forward and said, "We must be on time, Mr. President. The Prime Minister of Sweden will be in attendance." "Oh, is he? Oh, wonderful…" I said. I slapped the guard. "You can pass that along to His Excellency. With warm regards, of course." Adrenaline bounced through my body. Suddenly, I was fully erect. I looked at Darla and asked, "What's my speech about?" She said, "Infrastructure." Her fingers passed over her pearls, and I knew she was just as excited as I was. "Let the Secretary of Transportation handle it," I said to my detail. "He's been angling for my job, anyway. Let him have a field day." Darla undid my silk tie and I unhooked her necklace. She looked into my eyes and I looked into hers. They were so rich, so soulful. I was completely absorbed by their majestic, rolling mountains, their shimmering, crystal blue lakes...

Infinity Haiku

It was a summer night and I was feeling bored and listless, so I stepped out on the back patio with my legal pad and my cocktail. I was intent on writing a poem about the moon. That night, it was round and massive in the dark blue sky, with a slightly jaundiced tinge. Still, it was magnificent. I sat in a chair and listened to the frogs making frog noises in the nearby pond, the cicadas dutifully buzzing, invisible in the dense shroud of night. When I felt connected to nature, I put pen to paper and wrote, *Oh, solitude, the purest medicine there is...* Suddenly, a voice from above said, "Listen. Before you go any further, I want you to know there's a queue for folks writing poems about the moon. You must take a number and wait your turn." I looked up and saw a gnome sitting in a tree. I scanned my surroundings. My first thought, for whatever reason, was that I'd been circled by a small battalion of gnomes, hiding in the bushes and behind trees, waiting to ambush me and take away my pen and pad, then perhaps tie me up and perform a ritual sacrifice. I said, "Excuse me, but I don't see anyone else writing poems." The gnome replied, "The cicadas are writing their poems presently. The frogs are warming up to write their poems here in a minute or two. They have standing appointments." "Alright," I said, "I don't mind waiting." "The queue does not end there," the gnome said. "After the frogs it will be the constellations, one by one, beginning with Andromeda and ending with Vulpecula. You should know, as well, it takes a while for Sagittarius to get to the point." Feeling vexed, I sighed. "Let me guess, after the constellations the sun will have its turn, since it will be rising. And after the sun, the morning dew will write its poem, then the roosters, then the breeze in the trees, all day, until the cicadas have their turn again." The gnome smiled. His teeth glowed like embers in the odd light of the yellow moon. "Now you're getting the hang of it."

Import

My dog Rosie had just died and I was feeling lonesome, so I drove to the pet store, a big box store embedded in a row of big box stores. I walked down the dog aisle, looked at their pitiful, expectant faces. Some had beautiful spots. Others had floppy ears and strings of drool swinging from the edges of their mouths like a pendulum. Such beautiful, innocent creatures. It reminded me too much of Rosie, so I moved to the hamster aisle. Their faces were less impactful, with their beady eyes and twitching mouths. I imagined waking up with a hamster sitting on my chest, staring me down like a nun. It spooked me. The fish were not much to look at, either, and I skipped over the cat aisle entirely. Cats spook me more than hamsters. They always seem to be plotting something. I can't trust them. I shuffled on to the reptile aisle and said, "This is more my scene." I admired the turtles, calm and poised, and the stoic iguanas with their crazy hairdos. A man standing a few feet away beckoned me over. "You've got to see this," he said. He was standing in front of a terrarium which held a pile of typewritten pages, bound by two crisscrossed twine strings. "Is that a novel?" I asked. "Even better," he said, "it's a screenplay. Flown in from the mountains of Peru." "Impressive," I said, politely. "You don't know the half of it," he said. "I'm the one who brought it here. My co-pilot and I took turns reading it to each other as we traveled." I said, "You must be tired." The pilot's eyes were trained on the glass container. I took a moment to have a closer look at the screenplay. It was as still as a stone, the pages smudged and crinkled. Despite the pilot's glowing words, I couldn't help but assume this would make for a pretty dull pet. It didn't have legs, so it couldn't fetch or go for walks. it didn't even have a mouth to chomp on treats. Disappointed and confused as I was, I felt I should say something more, so I added, "Where is your co-pilot?" The pilot nodded towards the glass and said, "In there."

Suspension

I was walking to work when I looked up and saw a lake levitating in the sky. The lake was gray and craggy with ripples against the placid canopy above; it appeared to be shivering from frigidity. I couldn't take my eyes off the distraught form. "Do you see that lake in the sky?" I asked a woman waiting for the bus. The woman wore a heavy green jacket, even though it was only the beginning of September. She smelled like wet cigarette butts. A brown knitted cap sat on top of her head like a cocktail garnish. She said simply, "Don't insult my intelligence. Of course I see it. I've read all about it." I shrugged and said, "Forgive me. But this is my first time noticing it. Where did it come from?" The bundled up woman said, "Don't you read the news? It migrated here from the north, where it suffered religious persecution." I said, "I had no idea." The bundled up woman said, "Yes, evidently." Just then, bronze minnows began to rain down on us all. The minnows flopped around on the sidewalk, in the grass, in the street, on bodega awnings. Everywhere. Every few seconds, one of them would collide with my nose, or graze my lapel, before smacking the ground. "I assume you've read all about this, as well?" I said. The woman said, "I don't appreciate your tone. These are our kinfolk." The bus arrived and she boarded with the grace of an angel returning to heaven. The driver turned on his wipers as he guided the bus to its next stop.

Rebirth

A fallen rose petal lies on the hardwood steps of an apartment stairway. A mail carrier comes in carrying several parcels. She steps on the rose petal, and it turns into a purple pillbox hat. Not noticing, the carrier continues to climb the stairway. A few minutes later, the landlord enters the foyer and says, "My mother's pillbox hat! Why, that thing has been missing for forty years." He tries to pick it up, but it does not budge, despite how much he pulls and claws. The landlord concludes, "It must be nailed to the floor, in some enigmatic memorial to my late beloved mother. But who among my tenants knew my mother, let alone feel motivated to pay tribute to her? It's very possible this is all a jape to mock her memory. It's not right for this hat to be here, in this forlorn stairway, anyway, getting stomped all day. Pah! I will put in a maintenance order to have the hat pried up from the floor. Then I will place it on my mantle, right beside her urn." Satisfied with his plan, the landlord bounds up the stairs to post an eviction notice. A trio of boisterous children pass him on the way down. Their chaotic footfalls bounce off the purple pillbox hat, causing it to transform first into a yo-yo, then into a paddleboard, then, finally, into the trembling, beating heart of Saint Augustine.

Bookends

A man had some extra shelf space, and since his books had a habit of leaning, he decided he would take out his gallbladder and use it as a bookend. The procedure was fairly straightforward. He used a steak knife and a pink baby spoon to extract the organ, examining himself in front of the bathroom mirror. He was slightly disappointed at the size of the useless organ — the thing could barely buttress a leaf, let alone a row of hefty volumes. He tossed it in the trash bin without rinsing it, and again plunged his hand into his abdominal cavity. This time, he scooped out his liver. He had been a teetotaler all his life, so he supposed he wouldn't miss the mahogany-hued organ too much. He rinsed the liver, patted it dry, then went back to the bookcase and wedged it in at the end of the shelf, beside an edition of Chekhov's stories. The man crossed his arms and silently admired his handiwork for several minutes, as the liver shimmered in the late afternoon sunlight. After some time, the man's daughter entered his study with bloody hands, holding a small wet sac. "Father," she said, "what's this?" The man smiled and led his daughter to her bedroom, where she had a small bookcase of her own in the corner, filled with little books about wizards, fairies, talking animals, and shamans.

Acknowledgements

Grateful acknowledgement is made to the following publications in which portions of this collection previously appeared:

As It Ought To Be Magazine: "Slippage"
CC Zine: "Your New Liver"
Horns (Bullshit Lit): "Sex and the Opera"
The Laurel Review: "The Eyes Above," "Small Spaces"
Litro: "The Satirist"
Moria: "Coughing Fit," "Elvis Pays His Respects"
The Pointed Circle: "Diagnostic," "Making The Rounds"
Rejection Letters: "Elvis's Homecoming"
Retreat West: "Miss Lacy"
Salamander: "Elvis at NYU"
The Talon Review: "Surface Level"
Unbroken: "Bookends"

Many thanks to Jose Hernandez Diaz, Eric Jones, Dalton Monk, Ben Niespodziany, and Hetty White for reading the earliest, shittiest drafts of these poems. Your feedback and guidance have been indispensable.

I would also like to acknowledge my parents, Julika and Claude, my brother, Samuel, for being the most longstanding and earnest cheerleaders of my writing. Your love and support have been integral to every artistic endeavour I've embarked on, and I am profoundly grateful to have you rooting at the sidelines.

Lastly, Aubrie... you are everything to me. I don't know why or how you put up with my aimless rants and loopy brainstorming jags, often interjected in the middle of us watching *Shark Tank*. Your tolerance for non sequiturs is admirable, as is your patience and understanding when I'm at my moodiest and most cagey/impulsive/unbearable to be around. You never hold it against me when I just need to go behind a door and work through some shit. If anything, you encourage me to wade out into the murky waters of my psyche and get all of the brain gunk down on the page. You understand my mission, my calling. Thank you. Thank you. I love you.

www.ingramcontent.com/pod-product-compliance
Lightning Source LLC
Chambersburg PA
CBHW032054040426
42449CB00007B/1107